AN ENTITY OF CONTRADICTIONS.

AN ANTHOLOGY DESCRIBING HAPPENINGS AND POSSIBILITIES OF LIFE.

AF102631

T_R_A_V_E_L_L_E_R

XpressPublishing
An imprint of Notion Press

Old No. 38, New No. 6
McNichols Road, Chetpet
Chennai - 600 031

First Published by Notion Press 2020
Copyright © T_r_a_v_e_l_l_e_r 2020
All Rights Reserved.

ISBN 978-1-64899-062-5

This book has been published with all efforts taken to make the material error-free after the consent of the author. However, the author and the publisher do not assume and hereby disclaim any liability to any party for any loss, damage, or disruption caused by errors or omissions, whether such errors or omissions result from negligence, accident, or any other cause.

While every effort has been made to avoid any mistake or omission, this publication is being sold on the condition and understanding that neither the author nor the publishers or printers would be liable in any manner to any person by reason of any mistake or omission in this publication or for any action taken or omitted to be taken or advice rendered or accepted on the basis of this work. For any defect in printing or binding the publishers will be liable only to replace the defective copy by another copy of this work then available.

Contents

Preface v

1. Stilettos 1
2. The Bicycle 4
3. Uttarayan 7
4. What Happens At The Day When You're Left Alone? 10
5. The Good Ones 12
6. The Escape 15
7. Possessions 17
8. Steps 19
9. Wonderland 22
10. The Antagonist 25
11. Luxury 27
12. At Your Walking Steps... 29
13. The Girl 30
14. The Night Curfew 34
15. English 36
16. Lonely. 38
17. Time 40
18. How To Fit In. 43
19. Loser 45

Writer's Note 47

Preface

I think we often should have an outlet to express, to feel, to let go, and also to not let anyone else be hurt in this entire process in order to keep ourselves healthy and not indulge unwanted attention and/or guilt of hurting anyone from time to time.

In a nutshell, this was my journey to write these poems as a representation of my emotions and feelings, in countless, numerous situations I faced and pondered how they should've been. So, it's a creation of both, the true facts and how I wished they should've turned out, which you'll read as a typical perspective. We often come across situations and we always wish if they favoured on our side, which relatively seldom happens.

You will find all kinds of tastes here: sweet, spicy, sour, sarcastic, motivational and many more blended in a soup of genuine honesty, which will mirrorize you all in a way that some will feel to share it with others like a knot of mess untangled and celebrating it, some might not share it and cherish it upon themselves, thinking maybe someone understands them.

It's all about the human mind, heart, emotions and how we deal with them and sort them out like a pile of books in a library to their appropriate places, everyday.

An amalgamation of stories, emotions, metaphors, compressed into poems.

traveller

1. Stilettos

Stilettos running the path,
Striding Confidence on the facade;
The eyes don't stray from the front,
to below or above.

-

> She has the principal aim,
> Her ultimate goal decided.
> As if they'll ever know,
> They're just the pawns of the game.

They might be rulers,
Or some who claim to be her friends.
But they'll never know,
They're the guide to her success.

-

> She'll fight,
> She'll sacrifice.
> She'll be grateful,
> She'll quench people's eyes.

-

Her precise steps,
with a poker face,
leaving contemplation

on each one's gaze.

\-

> She seldom gives a laugh,
> about the day she always cares.
> How momentary would be
> the appreciation of her construct.

> \-

Her stories bled
in invisible strings,
getting tied around
her stronger, pointed heels.

\-

> If they only knew,
> how much it takes
> to reach the place
> where you can be.

> \-

She envisioned this
only took a lifetime.
To build an empire, precursoring
from nothing to scratch.

\-

> Scratches got nutritioned
> from the sources of anywhere.
> Almost halfway there
> to expose the success.

> \-

T_R_A_V_E_L_L_E_R

The process is processing
with or without her presence.
For now, she has to feed
the people's expectations.

-

                        Stilettos running the path,
               Striding Confidence on the facade;
                The eyes don't stray from the front,
                            to below or above.

2. The Bicycle

The bicycle knows its way
since 79,000 miles;
About high and wide plateaus
and wide and steep terrains.

-

> She's been driving it,
> From *Kanchenjunga* to *Angkor Wat*.
> *London* felt bad then,
> For it got so ignored.

Amazon and *Sahara* are signed next.
Ready for the expenditure.
What about *Switzerland*?
They asked about that.

-

> The sunny, bright sun
> and the windy clouds.
> Nothing ever compares to
> the sunshowers of *Australia*.
>
> -

Now she's in *Canada;*
Farming and Prancing in *Winnipeg*.
They asked 19 times about the *Niagara*.

T_R_A_V_E_L_L_E_R

And I didn't forget about that.

\-

>Then there's *Japan* to be at.
>All Kimonos and Noodles.
>Legs folded and eating with Chopsticks,
>she felt a different world.

>\-

Oh, don't ask me
how did she do it;
Crossing oceans and boundaries
on a single whim.

\-

>There are stories beneath
>this luxury
>of going anywhere
>in a single seat.

>\-

All those struggles and meets
for a unique dream.
Will be confessed once
she decides to spill.

\-

>"They" are the audience
>who asked me queries.
>"I'm" the narrator
>imparting daredevil experiences.

>\-

AN ENTITY OF CONTRADICTIONS.

"You're" the reader
who's enjoying this.
"She's" the brave cyclist
who doesn't know about this.

3. Uttarayan

Soaring blue sky...
Lightest hue and breeze white;
Anticipating colors of kites,
and *manjha* to link with the world bright!

-

> We've got the brightest sun at our side,
> the battle opponents on the other,
> It's already 7:00AM to begin with,
> Ready with our best *manjha*
> handmade from Ahmedabad!

-

My mother made *Chikkis* and *Laddoos* of *Mamra*,
accompanied by my sister for the *phirki* for now.
They're already having at it!
And I won't let them.
For my kite is attractive and stronger
Than the others like my skill!

-

> "*Ae Jaay!*" exclaims the victory side!
> *Pipudis* and shouts get wilder,
> making it feel as if we won the match!

-

None of the wins are greater than the first,

AN ENTITY OF CONTRADICTIONS.

because you fight and win and lose at the same time.
Like the bruises and the cuts on my fingers;
The pain, filled with victory,
decorated with adhesive tapes.

-

>The battle is on,
>afternoon and evening.
>It won't end without a bet won by one.
>The chase between the simultaneous wins,
>Atlast, comes the moment,
>The battle of sudden death,
>where we get the winner of this year!

>-

But it's least of our worries,
We enjoyed a lot.
We don't spend these days,
Like we used to prior.
Now, we meet when we can,
Making time for us.
Once in a while or twice in a year.

-

>I often mark this day,
>A souvenir in my entry...
>Every year, a new memory,
>A yearn for new longing.

>-

"This was memorable..."

T_R_A_V_E_L_L_E_R

I sigh to the sky,
"I hope you remember me,
After today."

4. What Happens At The Day When You're Left Alone?

What happens at the day,
When you are left alone?
Will you be happy or sad?
Or will you celebrate to the bone?

-

                        Some people find it pleasing,
                        Some people find it cursed.
                        Depends on how you consume the fact,
                        Of having free will innumerous.

                        -

They say it's sad and lonely,
To have no one to be with
Or you could find precious peace,
To have no one to share with.

-

                        You could be a miserable whiner,
                        You could be a jolly friend.
                        Why would you care about
                        Sharing your couch of candies?

                        -

TRAVELLER

What happens at the day,
When you are left alone?
A desperate might find his love,
The content might forget the world.

5. The Good Ones

I'm always jealous of those
Who are considered as the good ones;
Why do we tend to be at the back of them?

-

                                      They're appropriate,
                                      They're attentive,
                        How they manage to be updated.

                                                         -

With the explanations
people try to impart,
Gulping to their brains.

-

                                      Leaving us questioned
                                        The neutral ones.
                                    If it's all an act or not.

                                                         -

Even if it's all an act,
They'll professionally cover up,
With their high acting skills.

-

                                    I watch them walk and
                                    Ask a question,
                     "How is it that we've to accept their choices?"

T_R_A_V_E_L_L_E_R

Is it necessary that a single answer is
Mandatory for many arisen questions?
We could be who we want and
Enjoy to be.
Defeating many questions,
By an ocean of answers.

>They'll question your living
>Will advice to raise "standards"
>Thinking you live a life of the wrong deed.

But they'll never know,
The feeling of content
Ruling your busy heart.

>We've got to remove
>The stereotype
>Defining the good ones.

This definition
Has taken lives
In happiness and
In silence.

>To gray the area of
>Divisions of black and white.

AN ENTITY OF CONTRADICTIONS.

                              For harmony and prosperity.

The bad and the good labels
Want to disrupt
The peace we crave to bring.

6. The Escape

Is there such a thing?
About running from many namely beings?
Who once claimed to be,
in control of everything.

-

>Troubled if I'll expose
>their true nature existing.
>I chanced it to flee,
>far away to the living.
>
>-

I ran fast as I could,
being chased by three.
Fear, Doubts and
Obsessions of Negative.

-

>The escape is the faith;
>A door towards hope.
>Like a streak of light,
>breaking upon the dark room.
>
>-

I may have imagined,
a dot of white light.
Expanding into a garden

of happiness, visualized.

-

>Suddenly, fear grasped my neck,
>doubts holding my hand.
>I knocked them off with all my might,
>leaping towards the light.

>-

I jerked my body,
realized where I am.
I really overcame,
the battle of faith and hopeless.

-

>I glanced backwards,
>confirming they're gone.
>I breathed, "Never again
>will I ever be bound."

7. Possessions

A person is superior,
since the day he's born;
For he has many possessions,
the day he's on Earth.
He possesses his family sources, or may not but,
his birth day, death day and his abilities.

-

>			The only task he has to do,
>				is to live and thrive.
>			Although, he chooses to mourn,
>			for the things he didn't acquire.
>				And keeps himself in belief,
>				He has nothing to do but survive.
>
>							-

That's how he gets lost,
in the ocean of human beings,
with the faith of owning nothing,
but daily things to live.

-

>			Why does he underestimate himself
>				in such a wrong mindset?;
>			When he can't bring himself
>				to see what he possesses.

AN ENTITY OF CONTRADICTIONS.

Quite a hyperbole for the human,
who claims he arrives quite empty on Earth;
Having hard time to realize,
for what does he have but to
spend his next breath.

-

> It takes nothing but his one deed
> well-known to the world;
> Then the certain time after,
> he values his assets.

-

His birth day, his death day,
his achievements to the world;
Even the spoon he eats from.
Becomes the *Midas*'s touch of Gold.

-

> His belongings are very valuable,
> he knows it after his half life.
> We already possess these rare powers,
> treated like non-existents.

8. Steps

I saw my dream at the far end;
It peered at me from long distance then.
"Come hither..", it said.
"Come, get me.", it lured.
I couldn't help myself but it touched my heart.

-

                        Nervously sweating,
                          blinking numerous times.
                    I had to see, if it was worthwhile.
            If it could fill my stomach or my finances to care,
              I had to measure if I could risk it all to dare.

                                -

Decided to choose,
what I had to loose.
Eyes determined,
running towards the fruit.

-

                          The steps got higher,
                          Bold and numbered.
                          The dream went farther,
                          peering from the distance.

                                -

Can't give up now,

AN ENTITY OF CONTRADICTIONS.

this far I got.
The issue of necessities,
now, not the main plot.

-

                        Reached to the middle,
                          surprisingly tired;
                        Everything to achieve,
                    the dream beyond hurdles.

                                    -

Long time later,
blinking numerous times,
I saw my dream,
right in front of my eyes.

-

                          Years, Months, Days,
                        Who counts the process?
                        All they want to see is,
                    the dream in your grasp.

                                    -

The eyes that weeped,
The feet that bruised;
Having the time of their lives,
succeeded the long route.

-

                            The luring dream,
                              beamed at me.
             "You did a skill", it whispered.

T_R_A_V_E_L_L_E_R

"I seldom see."

"The dream is seen
by a thousand beings;
Only dared by those
who live precariously."

9. Wonderland

I'm a little girl,
who lives in a wonderland;
Far from the sadness,
dreaming about the best.

-

> Dreaming about how everything,
> waited at her whim,
> where she'd wear her glittery clothes,
> playing with her long, silky hair.
>
> -

Where she'd be served mouth-watering,
table-filled delicious food,
and wake up in the morning,
whenever she wanted to.

-

> She'd dream about her Prince Charming,
> How he'd abduct her to claim her as his.
> How he'd give her the world.
> And dancing with her all night, whenever she wished.
>
> -

I'm a little girl,
who lives in a wonderland;
Far from all the sadness,

dreaming about the best.

-

           From the happiness bubble,
     she considered to have a day outside of it.
        Where she'd watch the people,
           spending their happy days.

-

Strapping her knee-high boots,
and her favourite dress.
She departed her place,
decided to hit the coffee house.

-

        Took a long walk towards the café,
          with a happy smile on my face.
           Didn't realize the stares I got,
            I dressed the way I loved.

-

Jolly and Happy till she couldn't ignore it;
All the correct, bad comments about her
spread like the wind.
Fell first on her feet, making her a laughing stock.
She couldn't face the humiliation,
overcrowding her form.

-

            She wanted to run away,
              to go to her safe place.
                She wept so quiet.

AN ENTITY OF CONTRADICTIONS.

When she ran away,
no Prince Charming came
to her rescue that day.

-

New to feel lonely,
Never felt abandoned.
None to offer solace,
No one to hug.

-

Guess I'll stay in my safe bubble.
Atleast I'll be safe.
From being talked and humiliated,
I won't get hurt.

-

I'm a little girl,
who lives in a wonderland;
Far from all the sadness,
dreaming about the best.

10. The Antagonist

The wait was long.
We gathered at dawn,
with sticks and machetes.
The fight would be sweaty.

-

                    The din was loud,
            between continuous shouts.
              My fingers were shivering.
               The courage was lacking.

                                      -

Eye-to-eye,
unspoken threats lie.
A second was enough,
encountering lives.

-

                    It raised the hand,
        holding the weapon of a brand.
              I defended my armour,
              saved for much longer.

                                      -

The protection was on,
underestimated my power.
The opponent got tired,

fighting its battles.

-

> The win was legendary,
> to the eyes of my dignity.
> The fear got to its knees,
> giving up willingly.

> -

I overcame the fear,
by confiding in me.
With strands of hope and faith
within, a belief.

-

> It's the most powerful poison,
> left the beings with chills.
> Of all the things you avoid,
> Beware of the fear that kills.

11. Luxury

Don't dare to gush over
for the people living in their castles
have the happiest lives to spend than anyone
on this land has hustled.
-

                    They weep their eyes out,
                          broken and pathetic,
                            trapped in judgements,
          left wanting real, until nothing remains.
                                      -

Than the people with small houses,
happily baking cupcakes,
are the happiest to exist,
ignoring other ways.
-

                      Who's going to tell them,
                  they already live in luxury?
            Happiness, Family and Possessions,
                    what else do they need?
                                        -

A side of a coin,
played towards sympathy,
Selfish enough to tell them,

AN ENTITY OF CONTRADICTIONS.

they achieved everything.

-

>Don't dare to gush over
>for the people living in their castles.
>Trapped in judgments, left wanting real,
>Until nothing remains.

12. At Your Walking Steps...

At Your Walking Steps...
Your eyes are down.
Figuring out your path
to the direction you wanna go.

-

> One's unsure, insecure, distrustful.
> Or one might be
> processing, sorting, reconstructing.
> All these adjectives are
> written on your feet.
> It takes a walk to understand
> the purposeful grip.
>
> -

At your walking steps...
Your eyes are forward.
Hustling for the luxury
of the great future.

-

> Feet stepping sure,
> emitting glorious confidence,
> where you can see,
> The queen successful won.

13. The Girl

The agony burned
Till it was rage.
Tampering against the vulnerable,
paving wildfire flames.
-

                              Suddenly, it sparked fire,
                                  flaming the culprits.
                                  Once, the fire flames
                                  unable to extinguish.
                                  -

She wept enough tears,
couldn't stop crying.
The war was declared,
moving towards battling.
-

                                    The war began,
                          the deafening clamour.
                          Of the people to quench
                              the thirst of justice.
                                  -

The battle was disturbing,
from both sides of length.
Under the influence,

of impulse and strength.

-

> The girl stopped crying,
> couldn't tear her eyes away.
> From the sight she saw,
> bleeding blood on its way.

>> -

She begged them to stop,
when they didn't listen.
"Enough!", she screamed.
"I'm grateful for the protection."

-

> They stopped what they were doing,
> stared at her in disbelief.
> After she captured their attention,
> she started to speak.

>> -

"I want to fight my own battles!
I have my strength too!
Don't underestimate my power,
for a naïve girl, so bruised!"

-

> Stunned to answer her outburst,
> uncaring to wait for them;
> She turned her back from the people
> and headed towards the men.

>> -

AN ENTITY OF CONTRADICTIONS.

She walked towards the true criminals,
revealing her blunt knife;
They started to flee, looking at her,
she captured them in no time.

-

> One by one, she knifed them all,
> gutting through their necks in rage.
> They watched in awe, how beautiful she looked.
> Bravery, staining her name.

> -

Their lives left, her gaze intact,
with pride on her face.
Stared at the people, at each one's eyes,
oozing with grace.

-

> "This is how it's done.
> By klling the responsible.
> Not by killing the learning lead
> of false connections."

> -

People admired her bravery,
with honour and shared the story.
Told the girls to grow stronger,
to kill stereotypes and be inspiring.

-

> The girl never cried again.
> She always beamed with pride.

T_R_A_V_E_L_L_E_R

>They were always afraid to
>mess with her light.

\-

She, now trains the girls,
building the future.
For the girl should always
Be unstoppable.

14. The Night Curfew

Deafening silence is therefore upon,
the hours of the night till the crack of the dawn.
Exceptionally, the creaks and screeches of the breathing,
Crickets and Bugs await for the darkening.

-

>Oh, how I wonder it might be…
>Having a relaxed walk alone at the midst.
>Alas, like other people as me,
>got restrictions to not follow such a simple deed.

>-

It's a starry night sometimes,
or your blank dark sky.
From your windows to stare at,
with your blankets you lie…

-

>The silence is peaceful,
>after the rut maybe, as similar as you,
>is long forgotten and nothing
>to the gaze, many light years away.

>-

The night could go longer,
but time moves on.
Till it could touch and emerge,

with the rising light of sun.

-

                          And they dance and groove,
                          painting a beautiful scenery.
                          They invented this wonderful word
                          called Twilight.

                          -

It's fascinating to know,
that they meet only twice.
When the sun sets
And during the sunrise.

15. English

Oh, I don't want to feel this defeat,
supposed to be a moment of respect.
Of all the things, never had I thought,
It will fall apart at my feet.

-

> All the anticipation,
> all the excitement,
> all the things made happen,
> for that one moment.
>
> -

But oh, it wasn't her fault
for her correction;
She was only asking to improve.
For her what would've been better.

-

> But when she pointed out my flaw of pride,
> the one I am proud of,
> Oh, how I broke in front of her.
> In silent tears of wonder and shock.
>
> -

For the first time, I had an epiphany,
where I felt empty in my hands.
If I don't have anything to give,

T_R_A_V_E_L_L_E_R

What will I have to impart?

-

>Later some years, I had this contest.
>I scored awards in the past for it.
>But I failed twice both years;
>Their only fault?
>The concept they changed.

-

I couldn't prove myself.
How great I was and still am.
If you would just believe,
I would've proved it.

-

>Well, that's right what they say.
>If you don't get it after all the hard work you do.
>It never was in your name,
>And never in your fate.

16. Lonely.

This rain,
crying with my irritation,
interrogating my choices.
The choices which led me to this moment,
are enough to make me weep.

-

                              Even sunny days feel neglected,
                  with all the energy of ignorance and embarrassment.
Filled with desperation, transforming you into someone else.
    This is the test, where you choose to give up or be yourself.
          The battle between the want and the filled well.

                                          -

The betrayal is unbearable, I know.
It's easy to avoid than to experience and feel.
But it's inevitable,
a poison to die withering.

-

                              You find yourself staring at the rain,
                                      finding solace,
                                    a companionship,
                                       a friendship;
                          "Hey Sky?, you lonely like me?
                    Then let's share our pain together."

TRAVELLER

This rain,
crying with my pain.
A daily *traveller*,
looking upon me,
for a day.

17. Time

I'd be waiting behind
in your name.
Engraved in my brain
as a reminder.

-

                          That you'll reach the middle.
                                As a souvenir,
                                  to prove myself
                                    as a worthy.

                                            -

Why I always talk about expressions that
you impart on me?
You stage your reactions,
I know that a past ago.
So I read you wrong.

-

                                    It won't be long,
                                when we'll be apart.
                                Time ticks our steps.
                                Substracting itself,
                                beneath our feet.

                                      -

The distance we covered,

TRAVELLER

The oceans we jumped,
The darkness we fought,
The internal bleeding trying to heal.

-

                        If we'll fight our own battles,
                              If we'll be free
               from the threads that tie us together of
                Obligations that are mandatory to us.

So I left you at your home.
It's you who'll get crazy.
For answers,
we used to find together.

-

                                     Realize,
                        The craziness burning
                              in your heart.
                            For the answers
                 we seldom had a possibility;
         That we each other might have is
                   what we always thought.

-

That's why we sat on it.
With no agony of curiosity
burning us.

-

                          I hated that it was lost.

AN ENTITY OF CONTRADICTIONS.

>Lost on us.
>That we somehow,
>Individually, will find them.

\-

Our instincts were on rest;
For the mere presence of each other.
That they'll do half of it, relying on each other.
Maybe atlast, we'll find the road.

\-

>We were wrong.
>You can't believe in,
>A repetitive pattern
>fruiting no result.

\-

Here we are,
On the precipice of twilight.
To honour our feelings and obligations.

\-

For forever to come.

18. How To Fit In.

There's a need to be chosen.
A want for acceptance;
Then they'll look at you closely;
If you're ready to fit in.

-

                              The consumed breaths, packed;
                                They smell of the same air.
                                     It gets easier for them,
                              Identifying an extraordinaire.

                                                         -

No price for pretense,
For no one to know.
The sections of a person,
Split into more than four.

-

                                      It's such a difficult task.
                                        A character in play;
                                            Miming someone,
                                           That never did lay.

                                                       -

The walk should be the same,
Clothes as they'd prefer.
You can't dress in hats now.

AN ENTITY OF CONTRADICTIONS.

Unless you want to be talked.

-

>We have more rules to follow.
>An ideal to be an appropriate.
>Hoping we won't forget to question,
>the deserving matters to concentrate.

>-

It's not necessary to fit in,
if you like to stand on your feet.
And gossips and judgments,
Don't mock you deep.

-

>I've seen both kinds of people.
>And I've asked who's the best.
>The fitted in don't risk to look out,
>The rebel don't care about the rest.

19. Loser

Way, way far behind the skies...
I dream to go beyond...
From my school window,
Breeze reliving my mind...

-

                              A flying duster on my mouth,
                                  Not for to dare my dream;
                           But I will forever hate math class,
                              Or so they observed to foresee.

                                               -

I love my company with my tiffin itself,
And with my great natural buddies;
Rather I feel good to giggle!,
To see alienated stares of emojis.

-

                               Teacher gives me nil in Science,
                                    To be proud and honest,
                                       I'm a winner!;
                           Why they cry? Even if they tried?
                         They earned more than being a LOSER!

                                               -

I never do that but for them it's done,
And I receive revolutionary lectures;

AN ENTITY OF CONTRADICTIONS.

But I'm made of unbroken, yet those poke me,
And when I look around, world is a stage I see.

-

> When I make a list of all...
> I get differentiated from all...
> Though, I'm proud to be a loser;
> 'cause I'm the odd one out!

Writer's Note

Well, that was the end of this book and I hope you enjoyed this book and you can send me feedbacks on this mail: thisvoicehasit@gmail.com

Let me tell you about myself; I'm Pria Randeri; I reside in a nice town of Gujarat, India and I prefer to write under my pseudonym because I like and insist to be called by it and it's one major thing I'm proud of, as it unlocks a different personality from within when I write and many other reasons and it's one of the things I've done by myself and not by my parents!

You can read my blogs on: priaranderi.wordpress.com

You can also connect with me and stay in touch with me on my Instagram: @priyaranderi and my Facebook: Pria Randeri

Have a good day!

www.ingramcontent.com/pod-product-compliance
Lightning Source LLC
LaVergne TN
LVHW041549060526
838200LV00037B/1210